WE LOVE THE 90's

HODDER CHILDREN'S BOOKS
First published in Great Britain in 2025 by Hodder & Stoughton

Text & design by Cloud King Creative © Hodder Children's Books

Hodder Children's Books
An Imprint of Hachette Children's Books,
Part of Hodder & Stoughton Limited
Carmelite House, 50 Victoria Embankment, London EC4Y 0DZ

An Hachette UK Company
www.hachette.co.uk
www.hachettechildrens.co.uk

All rights reserved. No part of this publication may be reproduced, stored in a retrieval system, or transmitted in any form or by any means, electronically, mechanical, photocopying, recording or otherwise, without the prior permission of the copyright owners and the publishers.

A CIP catalogue record for this book is available from the British Library.

ISBN: 978 1 44498 263 3

Printed in China
10 9 8 7 6 5 4 3 2 1

The authorised representative in the EEA is Hachette Ireland (email: info@hbgi.ie), 8 Castlecourt Centre, Castleknock Road, Castleknock, Dublin 15, D15 YF6A, Ireland

WE LOVE THE 90's

Welcome to the 1990s, the decade that delighted us with Britpop, *Friends* and Tamagotchis!
As we said goodbye to the 20th century, the internet hadn't yet impacted the lives of most people, streaming services weren't a thing and we somehow managed without smartphones! Instead, tapes were played (and frequently chewed up), toys were beloved, bikes were ridden and memories were made. Despite the dodgy haircuts and double denim, we'll admit it, growing up in the last analogue age was pretty awesome. So, whether you lived through the 90s too, or just wish that you had, we hope you'll dive in to these pages packed with 90s nostalgia!

CONTENTS

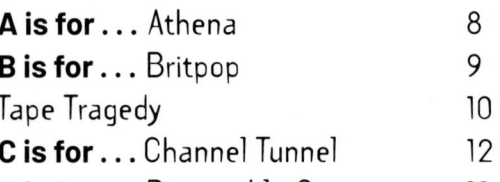
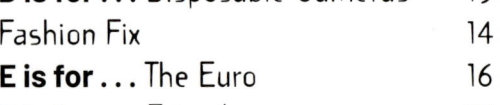

A is for . . . Athena	8
B is for . . . Britpop	9
Tape Tragedy	10
C is for . . . Channel Tunnel	12
D is for . . . Disposable Cameras	13
Fashion Fix	14
E is for . . . The Euro	16
F is for . . . *Friends*	17
Friends Zone	18
G is for . . . Gaming	20
H is for . . . *Home Alone*	21
Girl Power!	22
Super Six	23
I is for . . . Internet	24
J is for . . . *Jurassic Park*	25
Blast from the Past!	26
K is for . . . *Knightmare*	28
L is for . . . Labour	29
Battle of the Bands!	30
M is for . . . Millennium Bug	32
N is for . . . Nickelodeon	33
TV Hits!	34

O is for ... Ozone Hole	36
P is for ... Posh & Becks	37
Throwback Thursday	38
Don't Be Late!	39
Q is for ... the Queen	40
R is for ... the Rachel	41
Snack Attack	42
Scavenger Hunt	43
S is for ... Spice Girls	44
T is for ... Tamagotchi	45
Christmas Number 1s	46
U is for ... 'Unbelievable'	48
V is for ... Video Rental Shop	49
Word Up!	50
W is for ... WWF	52
X is for ... *The X-Files*	53
Classified Information	54
Next Level	55
Y is for ... Yo-yos	56
Z is for ... Gen Z	57
90s Super Quiz	58
Answers	60

90s A-Z

Are you ready to unlock some core memories of the decade that brought us both **Britpop** and **Britney**? Then join us on our journey in this **epic 90s A-Z!** From **blockbuster movies** to **forgettable fashion**, this is your complete guide to what was **BIG** back in the day.

A is for...

ATHENA

A trip to **Athena** (poster shop of dreams) is what Saturday afternoons in the 90s were made for! Flipping through the posters to see what you could replace your black-and-white poster of man cradling baby, tennis girl scratching bare bum or Che Guevara with was pure joy.

Beyond the classics, band or movie posters plastered the walls of most teens. And if Athena was too pricey, we made do with the 'free' ones in magazines.

NEVER FORGET! The Argos catalogue, boybands, Berlin Wall (fall of),

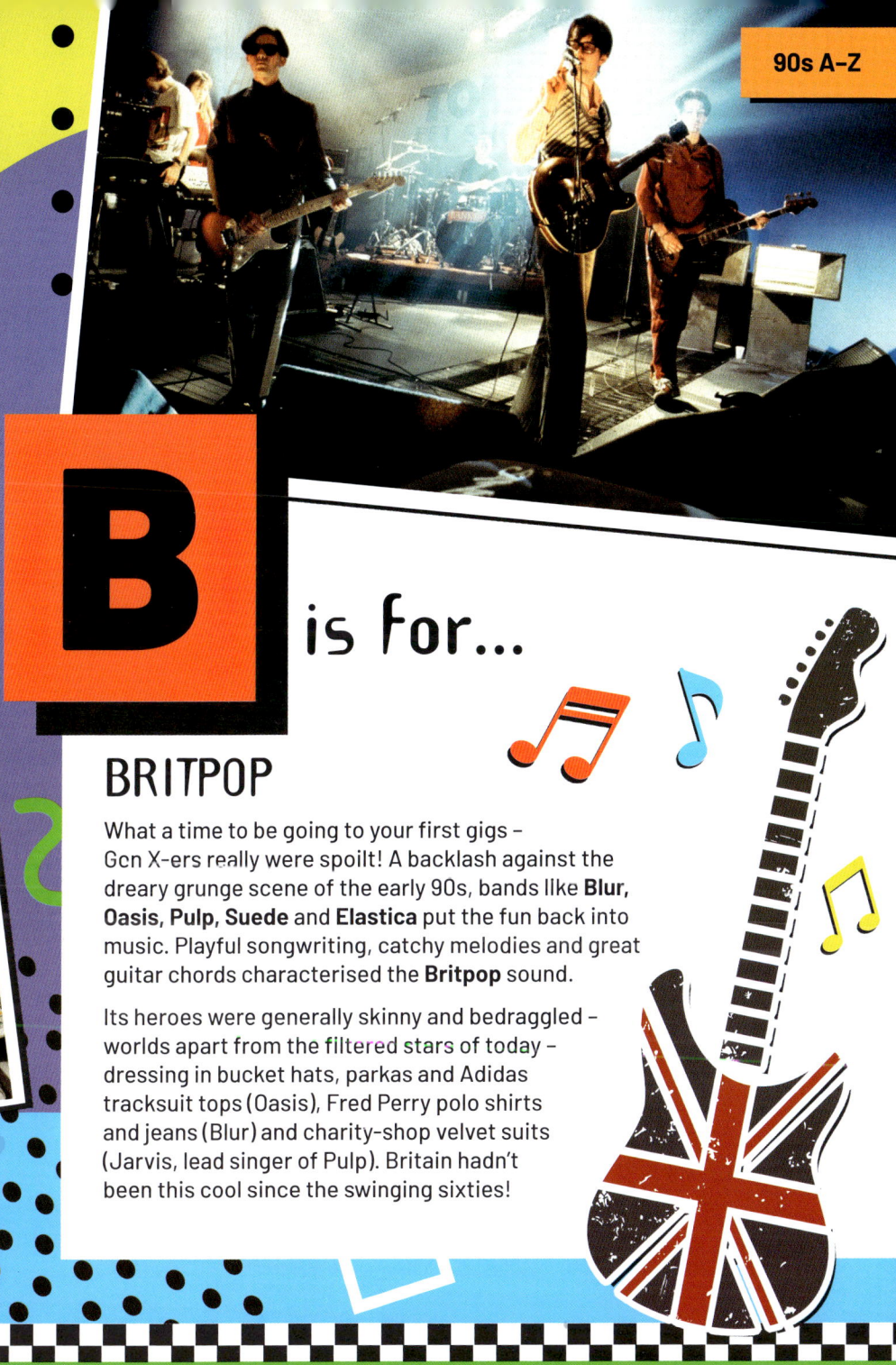

90s A–Z

B is for...

BRITPOP

What a time to be going to your first gigs – Gen X-ers really were spoilt! A backlash against the dreary grunge scene of the early 90s, bands like **Blur**, **Oasis**, **Pulp**, **Suede** and **Elastica** put the fun back into music. Playful songwriting, catchy melodies and great guitar chords characterised the **Britpop** sound.

Its heroes were generally skinny and bedraggled – worlds apart from the filtered stars of today – dressing in bucket hats, parkas and Adidas tracksuit tops (Oasis), Fred Perry polo shirts and jeans (Blur) and charity-shop velvet suits (Jarvis, lead singer of Pulp). Britain hadn't been this cool since the swinging sixties!

Billy Bass (a singing fish), Britney Spears, *Buffy the Vampire Slayer*, bum bags, Buzz Lightyear.

TAPE TRAGEDY!

Disaster! A faulty cassette player has chewed up this collection of epic 90s albums. Study the album name on the cassettes to work out the mixed-up artists' names. Then grab a biro and get twisting . . . **IYKYK!**

1

2

3

4

5.

6.

7.

8.

9.

10.

The answers are on pages 60–61.

C is for...

CHANNEL TUNNEL

The mind-boggling idea of a **tunnel** under the **English Channel** linking England and France was first proposed as early as 1802, but the project suffered decades of delay due to safety concerns and cost. Then at last the dream became a reality and the **'Chunnel'** opened in 1994.

Passengers could make the 31-mile (50 km) journey to Calais in northern France on a high-speed Eurostar train that travelled under the sea – minds blown! Queen Elizabeth II and the French President, François Mitterrand, were among the very first passengers to trial the tunnel, which celebrated its 30th anniversary in 2024.

NEVER FORGET! CK one, *Clueless*, *The Craft*, Diana, dodgy dance routines

90s A–Z

D is for...

DISPOSABLE CAMERAS

Long before the days of smartphones with their super mega-pixel digital cameras, **small plastic box cameras** designed to be used only once were all the rage. Once you'd taken all your snaps (usually 27 shots), you would pop the whole thing in the **post** or skip down to your local Boots the chemist to get your **film** processed.

The resulting photos usually ranged from *huh?* (the shutter got accidentally pressed) to good-but-grainy to completely charming! **Prints** were much more likely to be collected into a book of random shots, rather than the carefully curated albums of today.

('Saturday Night' & 'The Macarena'), Dolly the Sheep, Dr. Martens.

FASHION FIX

Fashion in the 90s was **pretty random**, while no one style defined the decade. Overall, the shoulder pads and wacky shades of the 80s were out and casual clothes in muted colours were everywhere. Mix and match **a look that screams 90s** from the choices below.

Headwear:
- Oasis bucket hat
- Blossom's floppy hat with fake flower
- skater girl beanie
- bandana

My choice: ....

Hairstyle:
- Rachel's layers
- Mariah's beach curls
- Winona's pixie cut
- Christina A's crimped 'do

My choice: ....

Bottoms:
- trousers & skirt combo
- All Saints combats
- Sporty Spice trackies
- baggy jeans

My choice: ....

Hair accessories:
- hair mascara
- scrunchie
- butterfly clips
- preppy headband

My choice: ....

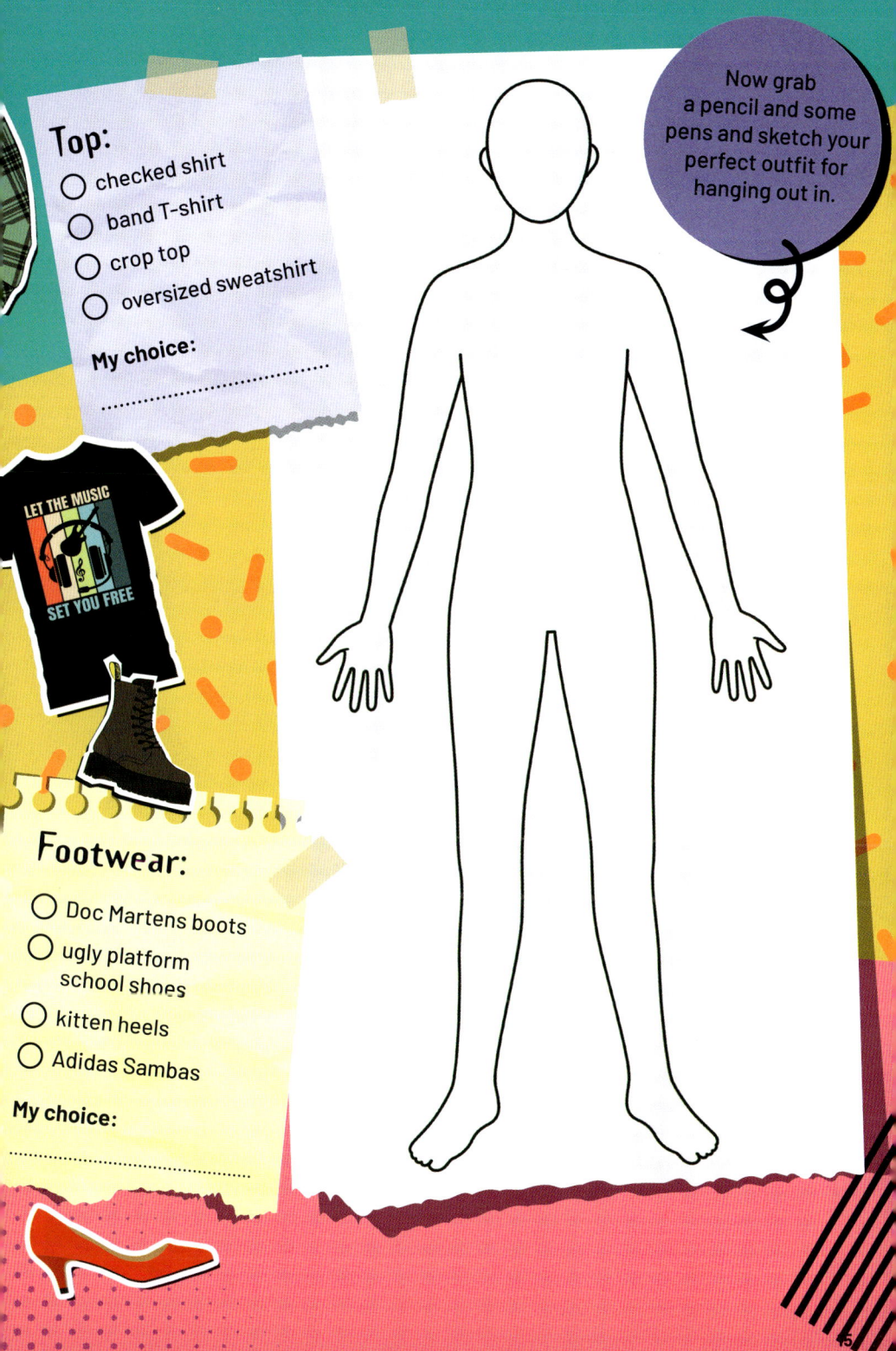

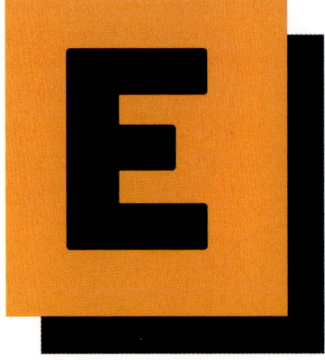

E is for...

THE EURO

The idea to create a **single currency** to use across many different European countries was first dreamed up in the 1920s, but it took another 70 years until the **Euro** was officially launched at midnight on 1 January 1999. **Eleven nations** gave up their own notes and coins to adopt the Euro, and the Spanish peseta, the German mark, the French franc and Italian lira were no more!

The UK opted out, deciding to keep the British pound, but it made going on holiday (at a time when cash was king) a whole lot easier. Now you can use the Euro in many more EU countries – everywhere from Andorra to Vatican City, as well as some countries' overseas territories outside Europe.

NEVER FORGET! Euro 1996 (when Gazza was great, but England still lost to

90s A–Z

F is for...

FRIENDS

The first episode of this **sensational sitcom** may have aired over 30 years ago, but *Friends* remains one of the **most-watched shows** to this day. Mainly set between the Manhattan, New York, apartments of six friends (just how did they afford to live there?) and their fave hang-out, coffee shop **Central Perk**, the show follows the lives of Ross, Rachel, Joey, Chandler, Monica and Phoebe.

Friends made megastars of all six actors, while some huge names guest-starred – everyone from Brad Pitt (Jennifer Aniston's then husband) to Julia Roberts. More than a few tears were shed around the world when the show ended after **ten seasons**, while a special in 2021 reunited the gang. Could we *be* any bigger fans of this sitcom?

Germany on penalties), floppy disks, *Four Weddings and a Funeral*, Furby.

FRIENDS ZONE

The one where you test your knowledge of the iconic 90s sitcom! Read the clues to help you complete the crossword.

ACROSS

2. The character whose job is a chef.
5. The title of Phoebe's song about a famously foul feline.
7. Joey's biggest acting gig, in which he played a doctor.
10. The name of Ross's pet monkey.
11. The city in which Chandler and Monica finally get together.
12. Chandler's single-syllable surname.

DOWN

1. The instruction Ross repeats when Rachel and Chandler help move his sofa.
3. A regular haunt for the friends, and Rachel's one-time workplace.
4. The US city in which *Friends* is set.
6. The name of Phoebe's twin sister.
8. The catchphrase of Chandler's girlfriend, Janice.
9. Something Joey never shares.

G is for...

GAMING

The 90s marked a **golden age of video games**, with some **HUGE games** and **mega consoles** released that decade. The graphics were awesome, matching arcade game standards for the first time. Sega's **Sonic the Hedgehog** arrived in the UK in 1991 with its super-fast gameplay, while by the end of the 90s, the first 3D platform game set the standards for all others – *Super Mario 64*.

Sony released the PlayStation, while Nintendo's SNES, N64, Game Boy and Game Boy Color were all next-level 90s consoles. Gamers spent many a happy hour playing **GoldenEye 007**, **Super Mario World** and **The Legend of Zelda** – just three of the decade's greatest games!

NEVER FORGET! *Harry Potter*, Global Hypercolour T-shirts, *Gladiators*,

90s A–Z

H is for...

HOME ALONE

A movie franchise that would never have got the green light today, **Home Alone** (1990) and its sequel **Home Alone 2: Lost in New York** (1992) were the Christmas movies of the decade.

Heart-warming and disturbing in equal measure, young **Kevin McCallister** (Macauley Culkin) is accidentally forgotten by his family who leave to spend Christmas in Paris. Kevin must defend his home (an enormous Chicago mansion – what did his parents do for a living again?) from dim-witted duo the 'Wet Bandits'. Kevin's series of elaborate **tricks** and **traps** to foil the robbers were legendary, while of course everything turns out OK in the end. **Home Alone 2** is a classic too (despite the Donald Trump cameo)!

Goosebumps, Girl Power, grunge, Hanson (of 'MMMBop' fame!).

GIRL POWER!

How many words of four letters or more can you make using the letters that make up **GIRL POWER**? Letters can only be used once, except for **R**, which can be used twice. Proper nouns are not allowed!

Find the answers on page 60 to work out your score.

1 ....
2 ....
3 ....
4 ....
5 ....
6 ....
7 ....
8 ....
9 ....
10 ....
11 ....
12 ....
13 ....
14 ....
15 ....
16 ....
17 ....
18 ....
19 ....
20 ....
21 ....
22 ....
23 ....
24 ....
25 ....
26 ....
27 ....
28 ....
29 ....
30 ....

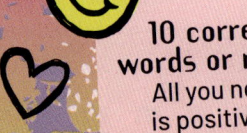

10 correct words or more: All you need is positivity!

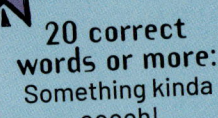

20 correct words or more: Something kinda ooooh!

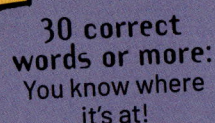

30 correct words or more: You know where it's at!

SUPER SIX

Read the descriptions, then connect them to the names of these six sensational girl groups.

1. A three-piece from Houston, Texas, whose queen went on to run the world.

2. A British-Canadian girl group who once split thought they would 'Never Ever' get back together.

3. An American R&B trio who warned us not to chase waterfalls.

4. Ireland's teen quartet who had four straight number UK 1s. 'C'est la Vie!'

5. A sweet-sounding band that had almost as many line-up as costume changes.

6. A girl band from Liverpool whose biggest hit made us 'Whole Again'.

A. Sugababes
B. All Saints
C. TLC
D. Destiny's Child
E. Atomic Kitten
F. B*Witched

The answers are on pages 60–E1.

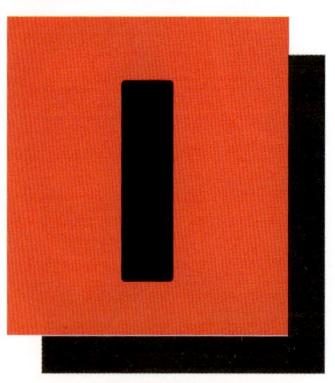

I is for...

INTERNET

Browsing the **internet** (or World Wide Web) in the 90s was a whole different experience. You had to get online from home, likely using a dial-up modem that connected to your phone line (and made phone calls off limits). Users clicked on Netscape Navigator before being treated to a series of familiar bleeps and scrambled noise, then their Windows PC landed on Yahoo or Hotmail to check emails.

By the mid-90s, internet shopping took off. **Amazon** and **eBay** were early trailblazers, but had tiny ranges and customer numbers compared to today. Internet cafes or 'cybercafes' began to spring up in the late 90s, too, as only about a third of homes in the UK had internet access. It wasn't until broadband replaced dial-up a decade later that life sped up forever.

NEVER FORGET! *Independence Day*, Impulse body spray,

J is for...

JURASSIC PARK

Another incredible film franchise that debuted in the 90s was Steven Spielberg's **Jurassic Park**, a series of epic dino disaster movies. Counting Sam Neill, Laura Dern and Jeff Goldblum among its star cast, it is set in a theme park where **dinosaurs** have been brought to life using fossilised DNA – what could possibly go wrong?

Packed with ground-breaking special effects, CGI and jump scares in all the right places, the first film was a global hit smashing box-office records around the world. Fans can expect to see more raptors and T.rexes running riot in the seventh movie in the saga, **Jurassic World Rebirth** (2025).

'Ironic' by Alanis Morissette, Jamiroquai, Jarvis Cocker.

BLAST FROM THE PAST!

Nineties bedrooms really did hit different! With posters of our favourite bands, an inflatable chair and for those super-lucky 90s kids, a personal TV – we never minded being sent to our rooms!

Look closely at the scene. Can you find **10 differences** in the picture on the next page?

2

Colour in a CD for each difference you spot.

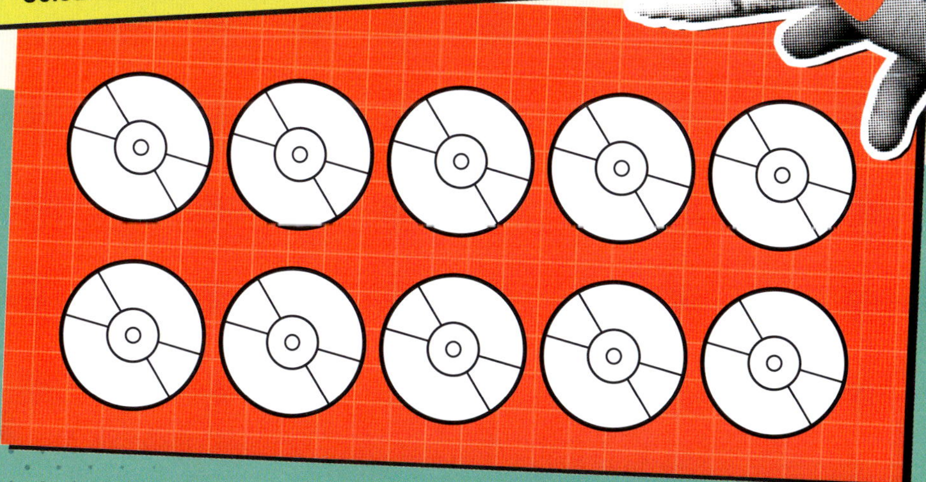

The answers are on pages 60–61.

K is for...

KNIGHTMARE

Arguably the best TV kids' show ever, **Knightmare** was a cult fantasy adventure that mixed computer-generated backgrounds with a team of real-life kids, or "Dungeoneers", who attempted to solve a series of puzzles in a medieval dungeon! One member relied on the rest of the team to guide them while blindfolded by the "Helmet of Justice".

The **Dungeon Master**, Treguard, offered the team advice on their quest, while the sound of the goblin horn blowing was enough to send shivers down your spine! Very few teams managed to complete the all the levels – just eight were victorious by the time the show ended in 1994.

NEVER FORGET! Kates Moss and Winslet, Kickers, Kriss Kross (why did they insist

90s A–Z

L is for...

LABOUR

On the 1st of May 1997, **New Labour** and its young leader, **Tony Blair**, defeated John Major's Conservative Party in a landslide victory, to form the first Labour government since the late 70s. It was an event that went far beyond politics, lifting the mood of the United Kingdom and renewing feelings of hope and happiness.

D:Ream's 'Things Can Only Get Better' was adopted as Labour's unofficial party anthem, while the new PM hung out with the heroes of Cool Britannia. Blair won three elections as Labour leader, although his popularity plunged when he supported the US in the invasion of Iraq in 2003.

on wearing their clothes backwards?), Kylie, lad culture, *The Lion King*, Leonardo DiCaprio.

BATTLE OF THE BANDS

Who remembers when the music press stirred up the **'Battle of Britpop' in the mid-90s,** when Mancs **Oasis** were pitted against Mockneys **Blur**? Definitely maybe? The best days! Whether you were a Blur buff or an Oasis afficionado, test your knowledge of these two brilliant bands.

1 Whose debut album was called *Leisure*?
- A. Oasis
- B. Blur

2 Which band bagged the Brit award for the best British breakthrough act in 1995?
- A. Oasis
- B. Blur

3 Which band made their Glastonbury debut in 1994?
- A. Oasis
- B. Blur
- C. Both

4 Which band is associated with Chelsea football Club?
- A. Oasis
- B. Blur

5 Which band had a guitarist nicknamed 'Bonehead'?
- A. Oasis
- B. Blur

6 Which song came out on top when released in the same week?
- A. Oasis's 'Roll With It'
- B. Blur's 'Country House'

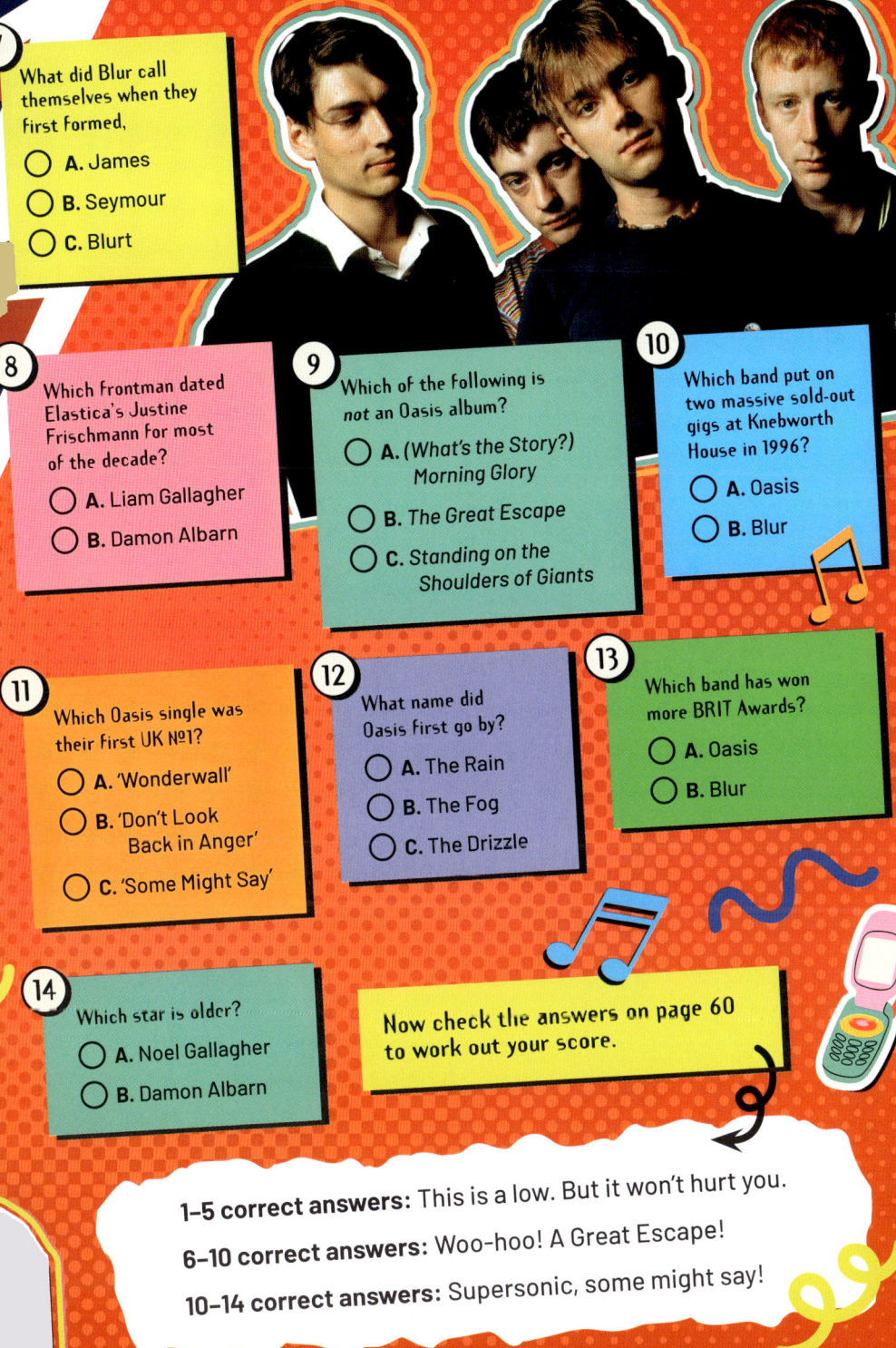

7. What did Blur call themselves when they first formed.
- A. James
- B. Seymour
- C. Blurt

8. Which frontman dated Elastica's Justine Frischmann for most of the decade?
- A. Liam Gallagher
- B. Damon Albarn

9. Which of the following is *not* an Oasis album?
- A. (What's the Story?) Morning Glory
- B. The Great Escape
- C. Standing on the Shoulders of Giants

10. Which band put on two massive sold-out gigs at Knebworth House in 1996?
- A. Oasis
- B. Blur

11. Which Oasis single was their first UK №1?
- A. 'Wonderwall'
- B. 'Don't Look Back in Anger'
- C. 'Some Might Say'

12. What name did Oasis first go by?
- A. The Rain
- B. The Fog
- C. The Drizzle

13. Which band has won more BRIT Awards?
- A. Oasis
- B. Blur

14. Which star is older?
- A. Noel Gallagher
- B. Damon Albarn

Now check the answers on page 60 to work out your score.

1–5 correct answers: This is a low. But it won't hurt you.

6–10 correct answers: Woo-hoo! A Great Escape!

10–14 correct answers: Supersonic, some might say!

M is for...

MILLENNIUM BUG

As the end of the 90s grew closer, the world was sent into a **global panic**. Why? The much-feared **Millennium Bug**. Also known as the **Y2K Bug**, this was a technological rather than a medical pandemic. The worry was that, at the moment the century changed, computers might not understand the new date and cause the computer systems we relied on to fail – everything from aviation to medical machines to traffic lights. It was over to the nerds to save the day! So what happened? Well, not much in the end. Very few teething problems with technology were reported around the world and most of those were swiftly fixed. Phew!

NEVER FORGET! *The Matrix*, Mariah, mix tapes, mobile phones,

90s A–Z

N is for...

NICKELODEON

Launched on 1 September 1993, **Nickelodeon** was made available to customers willing to attach a huge satellite dish to their houses and subscribe to Sky TV. The channel aired for 12 hours a day (7 'til 7), packed with live-action shows, neon-green gunge and **epic cartoons** including *Hey Arnold!*, *The Ren and Stimpy Show*, *Rugrats* and *SpongeBob SquarePants*. At the time of Nickelodeon's launch, only about one quarter of UK households subscribed to Sky, while the rest of us had to make do with four measly terrestrial channels. Anyone who did have Nickelodeon was a play-date hero!

NME (weekly music newspaper), Nokia.

TV HITS!

From **Buffy the Vampire Slayer** to **Teenage Mutant Ninja Turtles** (both sadly too long to squeeze into our puzzle), TV shows in the 90s were totally awesome! How many of these hits did you never miss?

	SHOWS	A MUST-WATCH!	HIGHLIGHTED IN THE TV GUIDE!	PASSED ME BY!
1	ALLY MCBEAL			
2	ART ATTACK			
3	BLUE PETER			
4	BYKER GROVE			
5	CHARMED			
6	CHUCKLEVISION			
7	DAWSON'S CREEK			
8	FRASIER			
9	FRIENDS			
10	GLADIATORS			
11	GRANGE HILL			
12	HOME AND AWAY			
13	MR BEAN			
14	MY SO-CALLED LIFE			
15	NEIGHBOURS			
16	POKÉMON			
17	TELETUBBIES			
18	THE SIMPSONS			
19	THE X-FILES			
20	TOP OF THE POPS			

Now look for the names of the TV shows hidden in the word search below. The words read forwards, backwards, up, down and diagonally. Which show is missing?

```
I T R P G N W B L U E P E T E R E R P V
K D E M R A H C H Y R Z O C L V G J Z G
Y A V L W F E R N Q L V P K B F Y L H L
A W T H E S I M P S O N S M E S R Q C A
W S L B S T C J K T R N T N V M H V F D
A O N R V Q U N U B A H R E P T O C H I
D N A H K L A B V E T Z F S M O Z N G A
N S D N E I R F B M G I N L G P T B R T
A C W T M N S R M I L T W O R O F Y Q O
E R P V H O M V T D E Z L N A F H K L R
M E Z N C E T H E Z O S Y Z N T K E A S
O E L J Y N X L B Q P U H Y G H B R E I
H K G T V C L F M V G C T U E E M G B H
L E K H P A G T I O L N F H H P G R C A
H R M N C H U C K L E V I S I O N O M N
T B V O R A X T L Z E B P S L P X V Y A
N A S K W H F M R B T S T Q L S Y E L P
Z Y A R T A T T A C K Y H I B V J M L C
M J N P L G V N S R U O B H G I E N A K
```

The answers are on pages 60–61.

35

O is for...

OZONE HOLE

The 'hole' or **thinning of the ozone layer** in Earth's stratosphere hit the news headlines in the 90s as a major environmental problem. Caused by CFC chemicals in products like fridges and aerosol cans, the layer of ozone gas protecting us from the Sun's dangerous UV rays weakened over Antarctica and other areas.

To fix it, an international agreement called the **Montreal Protocol** banning the production of CFCs was signed by every country in the United Nations. Amazingly the ozone layer began to heal, and if humans stick to the Protocol, normal ozone levels are expected to return by about 2066 in Antarctica and even sooner elsewhere. **Go, world!**

NEVER FORGET! (Atlanta '96 centennial) Olympic Games, pagers, pen pals,

P is for...

POSH & BECKS

The unrivalled **power couple of the 90s**, it was love at first sight for Spice Girl **Victoria Adams** and England footballer **David Beckham**, who began dating in 1997. The British tabloids couldn't get enough of this cute couple and David popped the question just a year later.

Their **lavish wedding** took place in a castle near Dublin in summer 1999, while the guestlist read like a who's who of showbiz. Doves were released, matching his 'n' hers purple suits worn and who could forget those gold thrones? A quarter of a century later, Brand Beckham is still going strong!

phone boxes, Pokémon, Polly Pocket, Power Rangers, Prince changing his name to a symbol.

THROWBACK THURSDAY

Can you find these groups of 90s gear in the grid below? Each group appears only once.

The answers are on pages 60–61.

DON'T BE LATE!

Late fees for video rentals were criminal! Make your way through the maze to return your tapes as quickly as you can.

The answers are on pages 60–61.

Q is for...

THE QUEEN

The same year that Queen Elizabeth II celebrated forty years on the throne, 1992 proved an **annus horribilis** (year of disaster) for the royal family. Prince Charles and Diana, princess of Wales, separated, as did Prince Andrew and his wife, Sarah, duchess of York. Princess Anne also divorced *and* a fire broke out at Windsor Castle.

Royal scandals were reported in the newspapers almost daily throughout the decade and the Windsor family was rocked further by the **death of Princess Dian**a in a Paris car crash in 1997. Diana's funeral was held at Westminster Abbey and was watched by more than 32 million people around the world. The next decade began more brightly with the Queen sending her own mum a telegram as the Queen Mother turned 100 on 4 August 2000.

NEVER FORGET! Quentin Tarantino, Radiohead, Record of Achievement,

R is for...

90s A–Z

THE RACHEL

Hairdressers must have been beyond bored by customers asking for the **'Rachel'** – millions of women around the world shared this style in the mid-90s! The shoulder-length layered cut with plenty of volume was made famous by Rachel Green (aka **Jennifer Aniston**) in the sitcom sensation that was *Friends*.

Jen later revealed that she never really liked the Rachel as it took so much styling to get the look just right. It made a comeback in the early 2020s, when Selena Gomez lent her locks to the Rachel.

R.E.M., rollerblades, *Rugrats*.

SNACK ATTACK

Draw lines to connect the lines from **eight epic TV ads to these favourite snacks of the 90s.** Warning! Two tasty treats are no longer on sale – look out for the red herrings.

1. Smart old Blue he took the _ _ _ _ _ _ _ _!
2. That Friday feeling – you just can't keep it in!
3. You know when you've been _ _ _ _ _ed!
4. Don't push me, push a _ _ _ _ _ _ _!
5. _ _ _ _ _ _ _ _ _ _... it's a bit of an animal!
6. Once you pop, you can't stop!
7. Full moon. Half-moon. Total eclipse.
8. Have you had your _ _ _ _ _ _ _ _?

A. Push Pop
B. Tango
C. Fruit Polos
D. Weetabix
E. Pepperami
F. Crunchie
G. Jaffa Cakes
H. Panda Pops
I. Pringles
J. Milky Way

The answers are on pages 60–61.

SCAVENGER HUNT

We're **bringing only 90s vibes** for this next puzzle! Can you find where the 18 stickers below are hidden in the pages of this book? Only icons that exactly match will count.

The answers are on pages 60–61.

S is for...

SPICE GIRLS

In 1994, Victoria Adams, Melanie Brown, Emma Bunton, Melanie Chisholm and Geri Halliwell all replied to an ad to audition for a brand-new girl group that would go on to take the world by storm! **Posh**, **Scary**, **Baby**, **Sporty** and **Ginger Spice** (before she split from the band, sob!), as they were known, had an incredible nine #1 singles in the UK, kicking off their path to super stardom with 'Wannabe'.

Spicemania began to grow around the world and by the time their movie *Spiceworld* was released in 1997, the girls had achieved world domination. They have now sold more than **100 million** records worldwide, making them the best-selling girl group of all time. **Zig-a-zig-ahhh!**

NEVER FORGET! Satellite TV & Sky Sports, scrunchies, *Smash Hits* mag,

T is for...

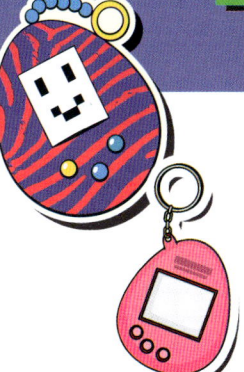

TAMAGOTCHI

First released in the mid-90s in Japan, **Tamagotchis** (translates as egg-watches) were tiny electronic pets that proved far more popular than the company behind the toys could ever have predicted. Three buttons were used to feed, clean up after and take care of these **virtual critters**, giving kids a first taste of how to be responsible.

The constant bleeping when your Tamagotchi wanted your attention wasn't for everyone, though, and no one prepared us for when our beloved Tama entered **cyber-heaven** due to neglect – it was enough to put people off parenting for good!

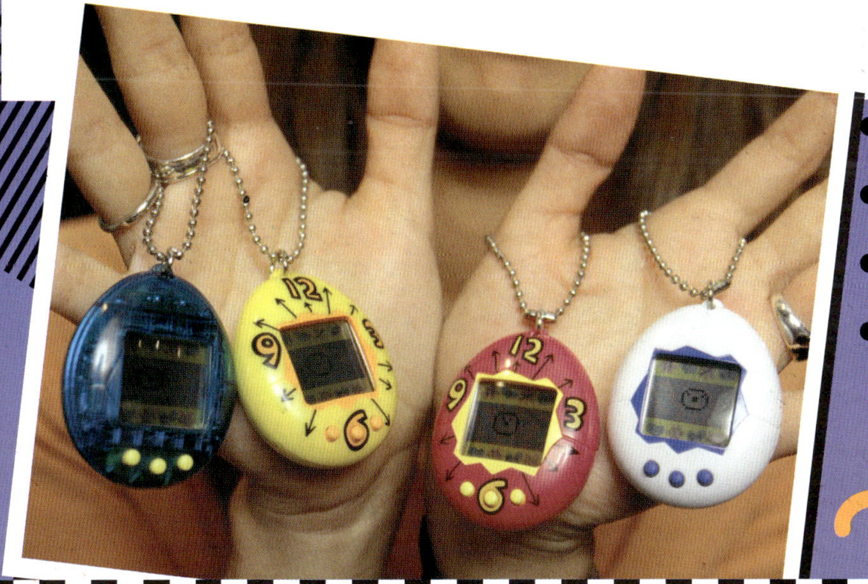

Sunny Delight, supermodels, Swatch watches, Take That, TMNT, *Teletubbies*, *Titanic*, *Toy Story*.

CHRISTMAS NUMBER 1s

"**It's Thursday night, it's seven o'clock, it's *Top of the Pops!*** " was the phrase pop fans waited all week to hear. The festive edition, with a live performance of the Christmas #1 single each year, was a holiday highlight. How many of these seasonal hits do you remember?

1990	**Song title:** 'SAVIOUR'S DAY' **Band/Artist:** CLIFF RICHARD (ask your nan!) **Weeks at #1:** 1	This easy-listening track was Cliff's second Christmas chart-topper! It had a one-week-only stay at the top before being knocked off by Iron Maiden's 'Bring Your Daughter to the Slaughter'. Festive!	**MY RATING:** 👍 or 👎 holiday hit / festive flop
1991	**Title:** 'BOHEMIAN RHAPSODY'/'THESE ARE THE DAYS OF OUR LIVES' **Band/Artist:** QUEEN **Weeks at #1:** 5	Originally a #1 in the 70s, 'Bohemian Rhapsody' was re-released to commemorate the sad passing of rock legend Freddie Mercury a month before Xmas 91. An amazing mash-up of opera, ballad and rock, the track is hailed as one of the greatest songs of all time.	**MY RATING:** 👍 or 👎 holiday hit / festive flop
1992	**Title:** 'I WILL ALWAYS LOVE YOU' **Band/Artist:** WHITNEY HOUSTON **Weeks at #1:** 10	A hit first time around for country icon Dolly Parton, Whitney's version was a poignant pop-ballad. The track featured in the movie *The Bodyguard*, in which Whitney starred alongside Kevin Costner and sold more than 24 million copies worldwide.	**MY RATING:** 👍 or 👎 holiday hit / festive flop
1993	**Title:** 'MR BLOBBY' **Band/Artist:** MR BLOBBY **Weeks at #1:** 3	The awful earworm 'Mr Blobby' wobbled its way to #1 ahead of Take That's 'Babe'. The novelty hit, often named among the worst songs ever written, celebrated the blancmange-like character of the same name from 90s TV show *Noel's House Party*.	**MY RATING:** 👍 or 👎 holiday hit / festive flop

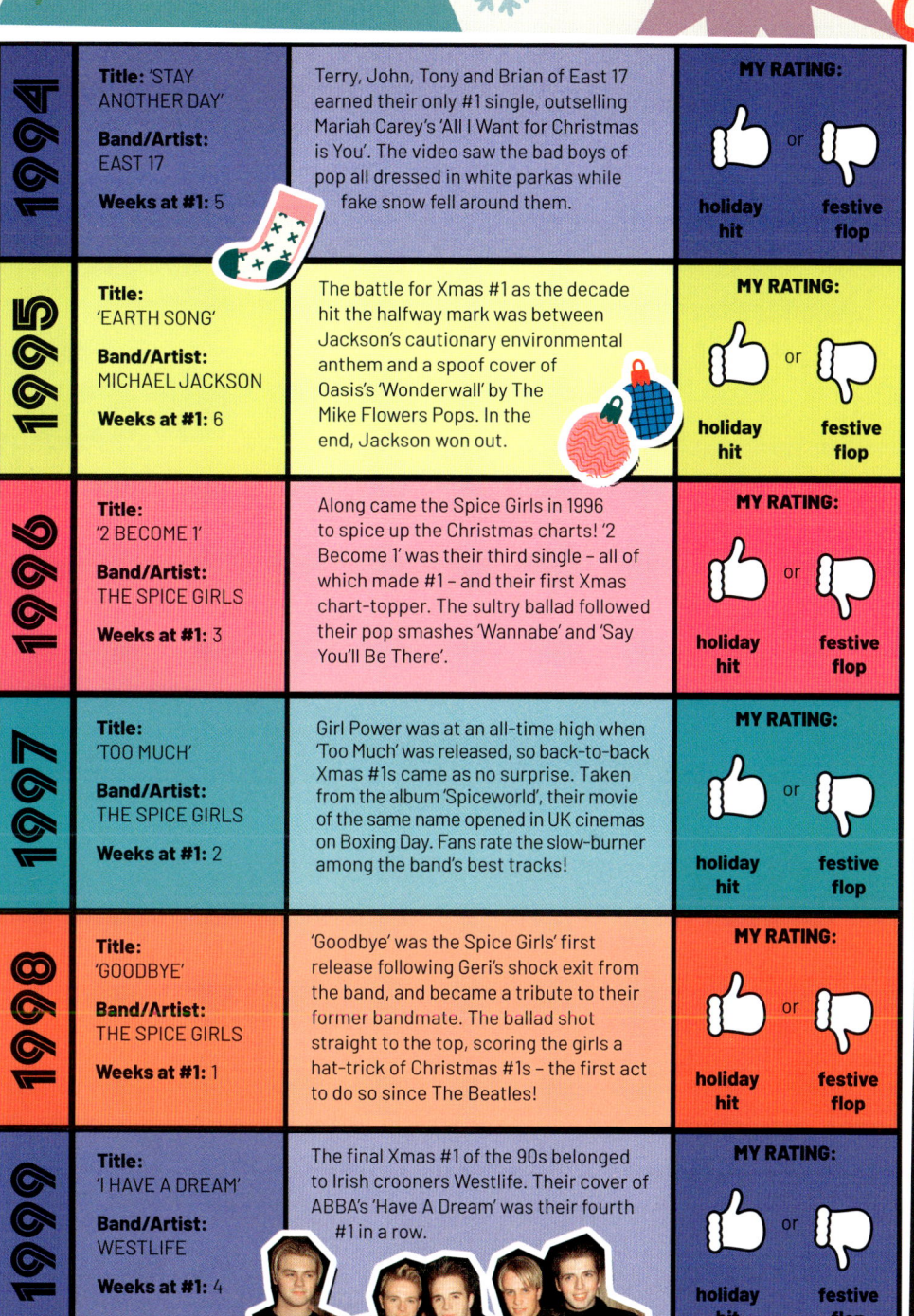

1994
Title: 'STAY ANOTHER DAY'
Band/Artist: EAST 17
Weeks at #1: 5

Terry, John, Tony and Brian of East 17 earned their only #1 single, outselling Mariah Carey's 'All I Want for Christmas is You'. The video saw the bad boys of pop all dressed in white parkas while fake snow fell around them.

MY RATING: 👍 or 👎 — holiday hit / festive flop

1995
Title: 'EARTH SONG'
Band/Artist: MICHAEL JACKSON
Weeks at #1: 6

The battle for Xmas #1 as the decade hit the halfway mark was between Jackson's cautionary environmental anthem and a spoof cover of Oasis's 'Wonderwall' by The Mike Flowers Pops. In the end, Jackson won out.

MY RATING: 👍 or 👎 — holiday hit / festive flop

1996
Title: '2 BECOME 1'
Band/Artist: THE SPICE GIRLS
Weeks at #1: 3

Along came the Spice Girls in 1996 to spice up the Christmas charts! '2 Become 1' was their third single – all of which made #1 – and their first Xmas chart-topper. The sultry ballad followed their pop smashes 'Wannabe' and 'Say You'll Be There'.

MY RATING: 👍 or 👎 — holiday hit / festive flop

1997
Title: 'TOO MUCH'
Band/Artist: THE SPICE GIRLS
Weeks at #1: 2

Girl Power was at an all-time high when 'Too Much' was released, so back-to-back Xmas #1s came as no surprise. Taken from the album 'Spiceworld', their movie of the same name opened in UK cinemas on Boxing Day. Fans rate the slow-burner among the band's best tracks!

MY RATING: 👍 or 👎 — holiday hit / festive flop

1998
Title: 'GOODBYE'
Band/Artist: THE SPICE GIRLS
Weeks at #1: 1

'Goodbye' was the Spice Girls' first release following Geri's shock exit from the band, and became a tribute to their former bandmate. The ballad shot straight to the top, scoring the girls a hat-trick of Christmas #1s – the first act to do so since The Beatles!

MY RATING: 👍 or 👎 — holiday hit / festive flop

1999
Title: 'I HAVE A DREAM'
Band/Artist: WESTLIFE
Weeks at #1: 4

The final Xmas #1 of the 90s belonged to Irish crooners Westlife. Their cover of ABBA's 'Have A Dream' was their fourth #1 in a row.

MY RATING: 👍 or 👎 — holiday hit / festive flop

U is for...

'UNBELIEVABLE'

Released in 1990, the perfect pop single **'Unbelievable'** by **EMF** was a smash hit around the world, and catapulted the boys from the Forest of Dean to fame! It remains the band's biggest hit to date.

But it wasn't the only unlikely thing to happen that decade – did you know that smoking was allowed on flights until 1998 in the UK? Or that many people booked their summer holiday via Teletext? Or that you answered your phone (landline) by saying your phone number? **Honest!**

NEVER FORGET! 'Unchained Melody' – Robson & Jerome's ballad wouldn't go

90s A–Z

V is for...

VIDEO RENTAL SHOP

Decades before the days of on-demand TV and streaming services, Gen X-ers and Millennials had the thrill of visiting the **video rental shop** to choose a film on VHS for family movie night. Customers usually had no clue what they were about to rent and videos were frequently chosen based on their covers, which made for some surprising viewing.

Rental fees were cheap, late fees were not, and leading chain Blockbuster's own popcorn and snacks were pricier still. If your luck was in, the previous renter had remembered to **rewind the tape** to the start. The thought of skipping home with a couple of tapes in their clunky plastic cases has us feeling wistful. **Good times!**

away! Volkswagen car ads – 33 million viewers once tuned in to follow the saga. *Nicole? Papa?*

WORD UP!

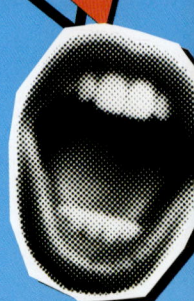

Complete these word ladders by changing just one letter each time to make a new word. Use the clues to help you! The first word in each puzzle is completed for you.

PUZZLE 1

#	WORD	CLUES
1	VOTE	What people had to do in the 1997 General Election.
2		Charles Dickens first appeared on one of these in the 90s.
3		The number of #1 hits in the UK by Bon Jovi.
4		What your Mr Whippy comes in.
5		An important or nostalgic memory.
6		The band that released 'Friday I'm in Love' in 1992.
7		The shape of Rubik's famous puzzle.
8		A nickname for the London Underground.
9		Blackstreet and Dr. Dre's 'No Diggity' was one of these!

PUZZLE 2

WORD

1. NAIL
2.
3.
4.
5.
6.
7.
8.
9.

CLUES

1. The surname of Jimmy, the star of *Crocodile Shoes*.
2. Diana Ross's penalty miss at the 1994 World Cup was an epic one of these.
3. The _ _ _ _ of the Berlin Wall happened just months before the start of the 90s.
4. Kylie Minogue is just 1.52 m _ _ _ _.
5. Jerry Springer and Oprah Winfrey had these kind of shows.
6. You might keep a pet fish in one of these. 
7. The piggy in which you put your pocket money.
8. Pulp, Elastica or Radiohead.
9. The verb that describes how David Beckham kicked a football.

The answers are on pages 60–61.

W is for...

WWF

One! Two! Three! Not to be confused with the animal charity of the same name, the **World Wrestling Federation** (now called WWE) was booming in the 90s – some fans even consider the decade to be the simulated sport's heyday. The world of wrestling was full of colourful characters, the costumes and catchphrases more colourful still, and the action had fans on the edge of their seats. **Hulkamania** was still in full swing at the start of the decade, while Dwayne 'The Rock' Johnson, a former American football player took over as the face of wrestling by the late 90s. Sky was the only place to catch the bouts, but plenty of video tapes were passed between UK fans.

NEVER FORGET! Wayne's World, "Whatever!", Woolworths,

90s A–Z

X is for...

THE X-FILES

The brilliantly weird sci-fi show **The X-Files** featured **FBI Special Agents** Fox Mulder (David Duchovny) and Dana Scully (Gillian Anderson) in the lead roles and had us completely spooked for most of the 90s. Whether it was a UFO, a monster of the week or something supernatural that the duo were investigating, fans knew that the real enemy lurked much closer to home.

Mulder and Scully's will-they won't-they relationship kept viewers coming back season after season (no spoilers here) during more than 200 episodes, until the show was finally wrapped up in 2018.

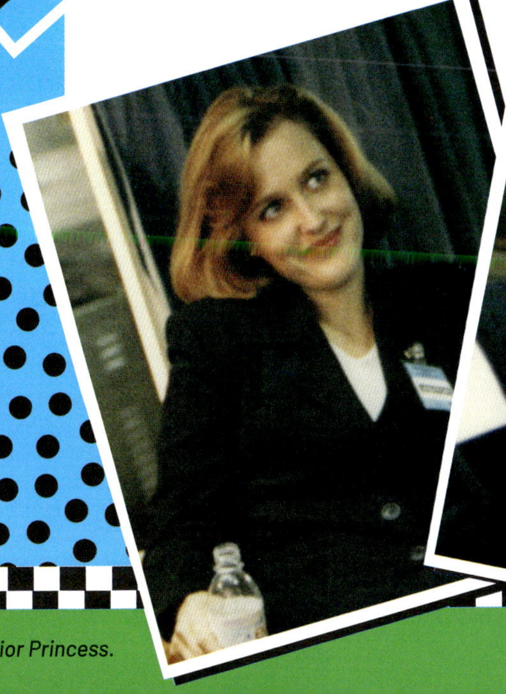

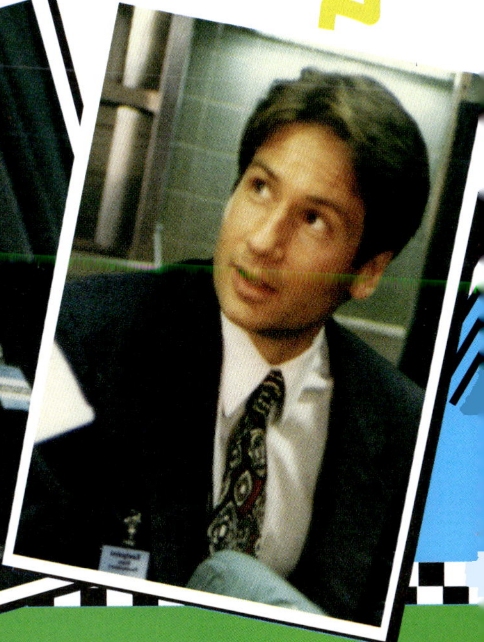

CLASSIFIED INFORMATION

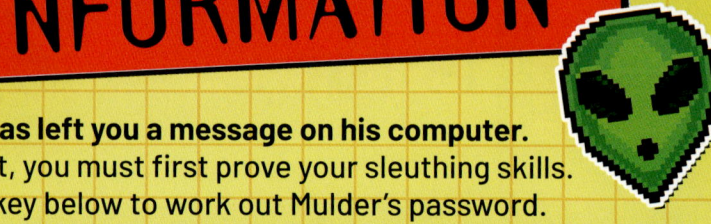

Mulder has left you a message on his computer. To read it, you must first prove your sleuthing skills. Use the key below to work out Mulder's password.

KEY

a	b	c	d	e	f	g	h	i	j	k	l	m
1	2	3	4	5	6	7	8	9	10	11	12	13

n	o	p	q	r	s	t	u	v	w	x	y	z
14	15	16	17	18	19	20	21	22	23	24	25	26

YOUR PASSWORD IS...

20, 18, 21, 19, 20   14, 15, a

GREAT WORK, YOU'RE IN!

Now take away one letter to reveal Mulder's advice to any new agent.

XTXHXEXTXRXUXTXHXIXSXOXUXTXTXHXEXRXE

The answers are on pages 60–61.

NEXT LEVEL >>>

The original black-and-white Game Boy went on sale in the UK in 1990, while the colour version hit the shelves in 1998.

When **Nintendo** brought out their **Game Boy** at the start of the 90s, some of its games were seriously addictive! Try your hand at this blocktastic game – can you fit all the shapes to perfectly fill the screen? They can be rotated, but not flipped.

The answers are on pages 60–61.

Y is for...

YO-YOs

Back in the day, **yo-yos** ruled! A playground craze of the early 90s, if you didn't know how to do Around the World or Rock the Baby, you must have been living under a rock! Professional yo-yoers even visited schools to show off their tricks! The ultimate yo-yos were branded Coca-Cola, Sprite and Fanta, with limited-edition shiny Coke ones in gold the most coveted of all.

The craze hit the UK, Europe and as far as North America and Australia and quickly fizzled out before a revival the following decade.

NEVER FORGET! Yellow Pages, Y2K bug, Zelda games,

90s A–Z

Z is for...

GEN Z

Anyone born between 1997 to 2012 (give or take) belongs to **Gen Z**, which comes hot on the heels of the generation known as **Millennials**. Born at the tail-end of the 90s, Gen Z-ers are unlikely to remember much about the decade, yet many are nostalgic for a simpler time, where music and movies were awesome, there was no social media to speak of and life happened offline.

First came fashion, then music, TV, with even 90s scents now adopted by Gen Z. So was life in the 90s really as rose-tinted as Gen Z-ers have been led to believe? Like every decade, the 90s came with the good, but also the bad and the ugly!

Zig and Zag on *The Big Breakfast*, Zig-a-zig-ah!

90s SUPER QUIZ

Are you a 90s nerd or wistful Wannabe? All will be revealed over nine nostalgic questions! Ask a third person to quiz you and a friend, then check your scores on page 60. If the scores are level, try the tiebreaker.

PLAYER 1

1. Can you name all five Spice Girls by their real names?
2. Which type of hat is associated with the band Oasis?
3. Identify this 90s tech:
4. Which year of the decade was the Queen's annus horribilis?
5. Name the actor who played 'Buffy'.
6. Which spiny speedster did Sega introduce in the early 90s?
7. What was the biggest environmental worry of the decade?
8. In which fictional Melbourne suburb did the Neighbours live?
9. Name Kate and Leo's characters in the smash-hit movie *Titanic*.

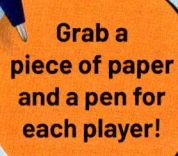

Grab a piece of paper and a pen for each player!

PLAYER 2

1. Name the duo of FBI Special Agents that compiled many an X-File.

2. What was the name of the most copied haircut of the 90s for women?

3. Identify this 90s tech:

4. In which year of the 90s did Labour form a new government?

5. Name the actor who played 'Dawson'.

6. What are the first names of Nintendo's 90s heroes the *Super Mario Bros*.?

7. What was the biggest tech worry of the decade?

8. In which made-up Sydney suburb was *Home and Away* set?

9. Which actor starred as Kevin McCallister in the first two *Home Alone* movies?

TIEBREAKER!
How many UK #1 singles did Take That score in the 1990s?

ANSWERS

Pages 18–19

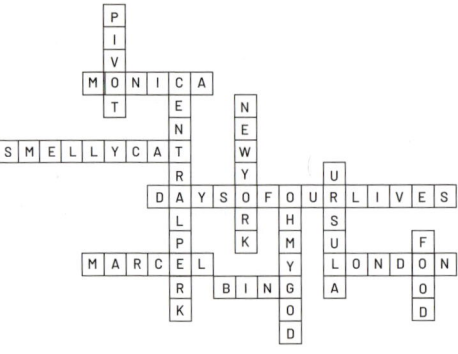

Page 26–27

Page 22

Note: there may be more correct words, depending on your dictionary.

8 letters: GROWLIER

7 letters: GROWLER, PROWLER

6 letters: GLOIRE, GLOWER, GORIER, GRIPER, GROWER, LOGIER, PORIER, PROLEG, REGLOW, REGROW, REPLOW, ROPIER

5 letters: GRIPE, GROWL, LIGER, LOPER, LOWER, OILER, ORIEL, PERIL, PLIER, POLER, POWER, PRIER, PRIOR, PROLE, PROWL, REOIL, REPRO, RERIG, RIPER, ROGER, ROPER, ROWEL, ROWER, WIPER, WIRER, WRIER

4 letters: ERGO, GIRL, GIRR, GLOP, GLOW, GOER, GOLE, GORE, GORI, GORP, GREW, GRIP, GROW, LERP, LIER, LIPO, LOGE, LOPE, LORE, LWEI, OGLE, OGRE, ORLE, OWER, OWIE, PERI, PIER, PILE, PIRL, PLIE, POLE, PORE, PRIG, PROG, REGO, REPO, RIEL, RILE, RIPE, ROIL, ROLE, ROPE, WEIR, WILE, WIPE, WIRE, WORE

Page 23

1 – D; 2 – B; 3 – C; 4 – F; 5 – A; 6 – E.

Pages 30–31

1 – B; 2 – A; 3 – C; 4 – B; 5 – A; 6 – B; 7 – B; 8 – B; 9 – B; 10 – B; 11 – C; 12 – A; 13 – A (6, while Blur have won 5); 14 – A, Noel (by almost a year).

Pages 34–35   The missing show is Frasier.

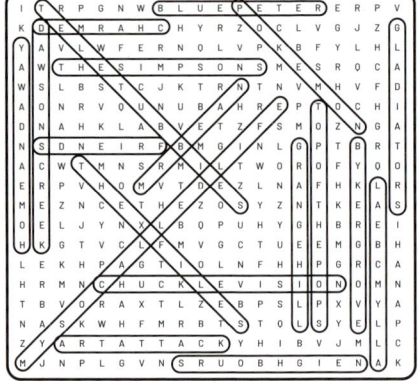

Page 38

Page 39

Pages 50–51

PUZZLE 1	PUZZLE 2
VOTE	NAIL
NOTE	FAIL
NONE	FALL
CONE	TALL
CORE	TALK
CURE	TANK
CUBE	BANK
TUBE	BAND
TUNE	BEND

Page 54

Mulder's password is: trust no1.
His advice is: THE TRUTH IS OUT THERE.

Page 55

Page 42

1 – J; 2 – F; 3 – B; 4 – A; 5 – E; 6 – I; 7 – G; 8 – D. C and H were the red herrings.

Page 43

Pages 58–59

Player 1: 1. Victoria Adams, Melanie Brown, Emma Bunton, Melanie Chisholm and Geri Halliwell; 2. Bucket hats; 3. A roll of camera film; 4. 1992; 5. Sarah Michelle Gellar; 6. Sonic the Hedgehog; 7. The 'hole' or thinning of the ozone layer; 8. Erinsborough; 9. Rose & Jack.

Player 2: 1. Fox Mulder & Dana Scully; 2. The Rachel; 3. A floppy disk; 4. 1997; 5. James Van Der Beek; 6. Mario & Luigi; 7. The Millennium or Y2k Bug; 8. Summer Bay; 9. Macauley Culkin.

Tiebreaker: 11.

PICTURE CREDITS

The Publisher would like to thank the following for their kind permission to reproduce their photographs:

Alamy: 8t Paul Adams; 8b T.M.O.Buildings; 6 & 24bl Seamartini; 28b WENN Rights Ltd; 29 David Gordon; 33t RGR Collection; 44l & 58t Featureflash Archive; 48b DPA Picture Alliance; 56b Model; 57t PA Images.

Getty Images: 6–7b & 18–19b Jim Smeal; 7b & 37b Dave Hogan; 9t Des Willie; 12b AFP; 13t, 20bl Science & Society Picture Library; 16br Ulrich Baumgarten; 17t Ron Davis; 20br Kristy Sparow; 21t Chicago Tribune; 21b Ron Galella; 24br Ullstein Bild; 25t Murray Close; 25b Yann Gamblin; 26 & 27 & 60tr Rodin Eckenroth; 30–31b & 58–59b James Fry; 31t Koh Hasebe/Shinko Music; 32b Avalon; 40l Tim Graham; 41r & 59tr Diana Gibson; 45b Xavier Rossi; 46t Brian Rasic; 47b Gareth Davies; 49t Chicago History Museum; 52b Star Tribune; 53bl & 53br & 59bl Acey Harper.

All other images not listed above: **Shutterstock.com**

While every effort has been made to credit all contributors, the Publisher would like to apologise should there be any omissions or errors, and would be pleased to make any appropriate corrections for future editions of this book.